#CREATEGREATNESS

Luther C. Green Jr.

DEDICATION

To all the amazing individuals who helped with this process. Thank you from the heart. You helped turn my vision into something I could hold in my hands.

"IN the beginning God created the heaven and the earth. And the earth was without form, and void; and darkness was upon the face of the deep." *Genesis 1: 1-2*

#CREATEGREATNESS

Presents seven ways to guide you on your journey:

Acknowledgments

1	The Supremacy of Faith	1
2	Preparation of Greatness	13
3	Inside Out	24
4	Intentional Intentions	40
5	Commitment to Greatness	51
6	Transcending Greatness	63
7	Sustaining Greatness	76

"The grace of our Lord Jesus Christ be with you all. Amen." *Revelations 22:21*

ACKNOWLEDGMENTS

Thank you, Lord, for the ultimate design of my life. Thank you for the victories, the defeats, and the scars. Thank you for the miracles, the talks, and the walks. Most of all, thank you for teaching me the ultimate lesson: greater is He that is in me than he that is in the world.

Thank you to the many amazing people who have contributed to my life and inspired me in countless ways.

Thank you to my spiritual parents: Bishop Larry A. and Prophetess Shelia D. Harris, as well as the Bridge of Faith International Ministries Church.

Thank you to my coaches for giving me an opportunity to excel: Russell Greenholt, Floyd Keith, and Tim Stowers.

Thank you to my parents Luther Green Sr. and Cecelia Green for a lifetime of love and guidance.

Thank you to Cherish Green, my beautiful Wife, Helpmate and Queen for continuing to support and encourage my journey.

Lastly, thank you for reading this book.

May God bless each of you.

Luther Charles Green Jr.

INTRODUCTION

Every day is a gift from God. Your days on earth are not guaranteed and not to be taken for granted. Keep your head up every day and continue to have praise in your midst. It takes strength to get up when you want to stay in bed. It is an act of faith on a continual basis to keep striving to be better. Greatness is given to us all. It is hardwired into our spirits, but at times it gets buried under day-to-day stress.

Life happens and causes you to forget about your greatness. The weight of the world is heavy and will cripple you with weakness and defeat your mind, body, and spirit. In every situation, God can provide you with the revelation to rise above and overcome.

It is my goal that this book will give you insight on how to pull strength from the true source of empowerment: the spirit of the Lord Jesus Christ. I pray that the message to **#creategreatness** will inspire, heal, deliver, and breathe new life into you so you will never choose to just give up on life or lose hope. God wants you to be able to find the greatness in your soul, elevate your faith, and unlock your true empowerment.

I pray that this book will change your heart, mind, and life forever.

It is time to CREATE your GREATNESS.

Chapter One –

The Supremacy of Faith

There is power within you to achieve your dreams and become greater than you have ever imagined. Think back to when you were a baby, when you were learning to crawl and walk. How many times did you fall down and get back up before you finally started to walk? Most likely, it was hundreds of times. As you started to master the crawl, you then learned how to stand. Eventually, you took your first step. You were fearless. You were not afraid of falling, and if you did fall, you jumped back up with a smile on your face. You kept on stepping until one day, you could run. You already had so much faith in your abilities at a young age that you were willing to try everything and feared nothing. You were walking in the power of faith before you knew what faith was. Where did that faith go? What made your dreams lose power?

There is one key element to unlocking this power, and it is called belief. Belief is what will fuel your power of faith.

Jesus talks about the true empowerment of belief in Matthew Chapter 17, Verse 20:

"Because of your unbelief: for verily I say unto you, If ye have faith as a grain of a mustard seed, ye shall say unto this mountain, Remove hence to

yonder place; and it shall remove; and nothing shall be impossible unto you."

This Scripture states that faith is so powerful that even a tiny dose will enable you to move mountains. There will be nothing impossible for you. A seed of faith planted in fertile soil can produce a supernatural harvest. Faith is fearless. It's a powerhouse of your potential, and it's free to you, courtesy of Jesus. Having faith enables you to walk a certain way, talk a certain way, and expect things to go a certain way. Faith is a power that can sustain you when everyone else left you. God will execute from the level of your faith. It is your belief that sends a sweet aroma up to the heavens. If you are asking God for something and you have faith and belief in your heart, your request will not come back void. Just simply believing and holding on to faith will allow that dream to be manifested into more than you could ever hope for.

You are never walking "blindly" in faith. In fact, with faith you actually see things more clearly because you are no longer using your natural eyes—you are using your spiritual eyes. Instead of focusing on your recent layoff, you see your new position that God is going to provide. Faith is that feeling that causes you to keep pushing, even though people try to make you quit. No matter what you have been through in the past, you can find your deliverance within the strength of your faith. Even better, the power of your faith is transferable to anyone who witnesses your level of faith. If others see your faith shine in the midst of struggle, your faith may help deliver them from whatever has them bound. Faith is also comparable to the wind: you cannot see it, but you can feel its power.

The wind can move a boat; make a kite fly, and even power a house. Isn't it amazing how something you cannot see or touch can move objects into position? That is what the power of faith can do for your life. Just a small portion of faith can help you get that job you wanted or help you start your own business. However, in order for faith to work for you, you have to be able to work for faith.

James 2:26 states,

"For as the body without the spirit is dead, so faith without works is dead also."

Your actions must show that you are working in the supremacy of faith: You cannot be all talk. Having faith means standing steadfast in that faith in every possible way. If you are not showing faith, you are doubting God's devotion to you.

Skepticism and doubt will cause you to become stagnate, and you risk losing the true calling in your life. Sometimes, we allow the frustrations of our trials to weaken our faith and hope. Instead of pulling closer to God, you intentionally drift away because you are no longer standing on the supremacy of faith: you are only relying on your natural sight. There is nothing natural about faith. You must be driven to live by something you cannot see. It is often a struggle, but you will find out that if you just hold on a little bit longer, your blessing will reach its destination on time. It is like being the bull rider in a rodeo competition. The pressure of trying to hold on to something that is bigger and more powerful than you is overwhelming. The fear that you may be crushed if you let go terrifies you, but you climb on and hold on with all of your might

because you want to be victorious. Faith is no different!

You must hold on to faith, even if the weight of your

struggle is overpowering at times. Your faith isn't how

much you can lift but how long you can hold on. The

supremacy of faith is that even at your weakest

moment, you are stronger than you could ever imagine.

Whatever you dream about becoming, you must

believe that you are good enough to make it happen.

Remember that you only need one small seed of faith to

create supernatural harvests in your life. You can

achieve all that you are destined to achieve when you

have faith in yourself and God's plan for your life. The

amazing thing about God is that you can come to Him

broken with cracks all over your body, but He will heal

all those cracks and make you whole. You can come to God defeated, and He will make you a winner!

Greatness is in what you see, even if it is not something that you can reach out and touch just yet. There is a supreme power in being able to look past the present issue and see the future result. Martin Luther King, Jr. said it best when he said, "Take the first step in faith, even if you don't see the whole staircase." As long as the staircase is going up, even if you miss a step and slip, you will still be in a higher position than where you started from. Just keep moving, and don't stop climbing. An example of this is when Jesus looked past the pain of the cross and saw your salvation. When Jesus took on the crown of thorns piercing his scalp, He saw YOU. When Jesus took the nails in his hand and feet, He saw YOU. God had faith and believed that you could live a greater life through Him if He manifested himself in the flesh and died for you. God still believed in YOU as He hung on the cross. What is your excuse not to believe in him? Jesus will give you what you need to accomplish your dreams. God still believes in YOU, and it's time to start believing in him. You may not think you can hold on and do it right now, but you should never forget the one who can step in and carry you while you catch your breath and regain your strength. There is a supreme, supernatural power in your faith!

Never give up on yourself because no matter what, God will never give up fighting for you! Leave your past behind and never look back. On this journey, the things you conquer will be left behind you. You don't have to look back to see how far you have come. You will see it in everything in front of you, and you will

know it deep within your soul. Through faith, God will

give you a way out of bondage and show you the

direction to walk towards your freedom. Don't turn

back and look because that will show unbelief in the

power that is leading you out. Those things were left

behind you for a reason.

Luke 9:59-62 states,

"And he said unto another, Follow me. But he said,

Lord, suffer me first to go and bury my father. Jesus

said unto him, Let the dead bury their dead: but go

thou and preach the kingdom of God. And another

also said, Lord, I will follow thee; but let me first go

bid them farewell, which are at home at my house.

And Jesus said unto him, No man, having put his hand to the plough, and looking back, is fit for the kingdom of God. "

Do not retrace old worn out trails. Have the supreme power of faith to walk on a new one. Greatness does not waste time looking back, but it always finds a way to keep looking up. There will never be anything behind you that will help you. God places all things in front of you that will help you grow and become the great person you are called to be. You are called to walk by faith. Your level of faith will show God that you are ready for all that He is willing to give to you.

Having faith does not mean that everything will be easy, but faith says that anything can be done:

mountains can be moved, and you can conquer the things that used to defeat you! There will be moments along the way when faith may be the only thing you have to hold on to. Just hold on and allow it to direct you through. Fight the good fight of faith, and be motivated to create your greatness! Your situation can no longer stop you. You now have become greater than your situation! That is the supremacy of faith. It is time to grab a hold of it and never let go!

Chapter Two –
Preparation of Greatness

When your alarm clock goes off and you open your eyes to see the sun shining through the blinds of the windows, stretch your arms to the sky and say, "Thank you Lord for waking me up this morning. Thank you for giving me one more day to see, walk, breathe, talk, and another day to give you praise, God." As you thank your savior, my Lord Jesus Christ, look into the mirror, stretch, and say, "Thank you God for giving me another chance to get it right!"

Every morning you wake up is a gift from God, and you should be blessed in it. Never should you wake up and say, "It's going to be a bad day" because in a sense, you are speaking that bad day into existence. Would you ever look at your newborn baby and say, "This is going to be a bad child"? No, you look at that newborn and say that you are blessed. Every day will not be sunny, and some days it will rain, but you are blessed for the new birth of another day, even if it isn't the right temperature for you. No matter how prepared and put together you are, adversity (rain) will eventually come. At times, it may feel like everything is going wrong in your life. No matter how heavy it may be, it's not meant to destroy you; it's meant to prepare you for greater things.

Adversity is the preparation for greatness. When bad situations happen in your life, it is meant to give you wisdom. Dr. Martin Luther King, Jr., Rosa Parks, and Jackie Robinson, among others, all had to endure some type of adversity that tested their faith. You must maintain your spirit in order to respond to adversity, not run or avoid hardship. If something doesn't challenge you, it doesn't change you. Change is the key to spiritual growth. When it starts to pour down rain, do you just stand in it and get soaked, or do you make a move to get out of it? When it's too sunny outside, do you just stand with your eyes closed? No, you will adapt or regroup and move to find some type of covering. In the past, when the ocean became too rough for boats made of wood, they made them out of steel, a stronger material. This is how you should look at adversity; it is meant to change you so the new you can be made of stronger material. Adversity is the time for your body, mind, and spirit to become upgraded. Adversity strengthens your greatness.

Do you believe that you are worthy and capable of greatness? Greatness is defined as "a state of superiority that affects a person, object, or place." The unique thing about greatness is that it is already predetermined for you. Before you were created, greatness was already hardwired into your DNA. Greatness pumps through your body with every breath, every heartbeat, and every thought. However, as life happens, we forget about how powerful we actually are. Greatness is a state of mind, and it is the foundation you were built upon. It is something that is inside of you that tells you to get up even if you have been knocked down.

In the Bible, when Jesus carried that old, rugged cross down that rocky, dusty road, ready to sacrifice his life, He had you in mind. How many times did Jesus stumble and fall with that cross? How many times did our Savior keep getting up and pushing through? Instead of picturing Jesus carrying a cross, picture Him carrying YOU on his back. Jesus died for YOU. He gave up His life so you would have a right to greatness. He endured the crown of thorns as well as being beaten, spit on, whipped, and embarrassed. Jesus suffered nails being hammered into the flesh and bone of His feet and hands so that you can have the right of greatness. Greatness was His gift to give to us all. He had the greatness mind state because the greatness in Him was to become the greatness in you. When you fall down and others walk by you and talk about you, God will pick you up and whisper in your ear, "You are going to be a powerful person." God gave up His only Son for you to have eternal life.

In order to prepare for greatness, you must have a vision of being greater than you are now. You must believe that you are destined to be great and turn your dreams into realities. Your greatness has no boundaries or limits. Greatness is powerful and contagious. The preparation for greatness allows ordinary people to produce extraordinary results. Situations and adversity are meant to give you wisdom. There is always a purpose and a plan behind adversity in your life. Even in the dictionary, you won't see "greatness" before the word "adversity," "success" before "storm," or even "increase" before "decrease." When you are going through storms, God wants to see if you will still serve Him. How can God give you an increase if you quit when life gets tough? What you cannot see is that God has been preparing you for your increase. Sometimes God needs you to decrease before you can increase. If you will not praise God and still find joy in hard times, then you are failing to prepare for greatness.

In nature, storms are powerful forces that bring high winds, torrential rains, and potential destruction. If you take a look at a storm in a spiritual sense, these storms in life give birth to some of your greatest accomplishments. The storms of childbirth, your first break-up, the first time you were laid off and raising your children all have upgraded you and given you wisdom. However unfortunate, bad things can happen to good people. At times, it could mean that you're a strong person, and God gifted you enough to keep "fighting the fight." Sometimes, God will take you through storms so that things that are hindering you will be uprooted. Then you will have a clearer vision of where you are supposed to be. Remember, God won't put more on you than you can bear. God knows your situation before it even arises and knows exactly what you will do before you even do it. God has prepared you for greatness.

When circumstances start mounting up, your preparation for greatness is the most important. Become encouraged and press on because that temporary struggle gives birth to your eternal greatness. It is a process, but you are built to endure the struggle. Remember, every storm you overcome makes you stronger than ever. That is the preparation of greatness. The preparation phase may be heavy and difficult to bear, but you will be better because you went through it. You will never truly know what you are capable of until you are tested.

1 Peter 2:9 states,

"We are a chosen generation, royal priesthood, a holy nation, a peculiar people [...]"

What that means is that you are purposed, chosen and destined to show the world your powerful gift. At times, greatness means looking at your life now and understanding how blessed you are because you are still standing tall! All situations and circumstances are meant to help us grow into what God has for us. Remember that your trials are very valuable. If it was not for those trials, how would you ever be as great as you are now? You are greater now than ever before! Trust that your hardest trial will give birth to your greatest breakthrough! Use the strength that God gave you to speak life into every situation that arises. See the storms as opportunities to grow. It is not about what was taken away or shaken; it is about what was still standing and added. God did not build you to be weak. You were created to be strong. As a matter of fact, Jesus died so you could become powerful! You must stop proclaiming and complaining about your weaknesses and start celebrating your strengths and your triumphs!

2 Corinthians 4:17-18 states:

"For our light affliction, which is but for a moment, worketh for us a far more exceeding and eternal weight of glory. While we look not at the things which are seen, but at the things which are not seen; for the things which are seen are temporal (temporary/worldly); but the things which are not seen are eternal (lasting forever)."

Challenge yourself to always remember that you are

purposed, unique, destined, and created for greatness.

Greatness is having superiority over your situation!

Chapter Three –

Inside Out

If faith can move mountains and storms can bring wisdom, then what is holding you back? Why is your heart still heavy? Why do you still feel like you are stuck? Does your life consist of casting stones, or does it consist of building a foundation for your future? Do you believe you are destined to be great, or are you waiting to be discovered for your greatness? Is joy radiating from within you, or is the company you keep wearing you down? You must be able to see people for who they are, not just with your physical eyes but with your spiritual eyes. You must take a self-examination from the inside out. Your anatomical eyes can see many beautiful and great things, but your spiritual eyes can see deep emotions and things unseen. Your spiritual eyes can discern who or what something is by a feeling deep inside your spirit. God will tell you and show you exactly who someone is, but you must be willing to trust and act on what God reveals to you. What if God is telling you that you are blocking your own greatness?

First, will you be strong enough to change yourself? Sometimes, it is not what is around you that is causing negativity in your life; it is what is inside of you. If you have ever entered into a room only to see everyone leave, then quite possibly you may not be as fresh as you think. Right now, we are not talking about physical freshness; we are talking about your spiritual freshness. You can spend hundreds of dollars on perfumes and colognes to make your flesh smell good,

but have you examined your spirit to make sure that it

is a sweet aroma of God or a stale stench of your own

self-righteousness? Do you motivate others to excel?

Are you forgiving and trustworthy?

**"Just because it looks good on the outside doesn't
mean its well-done on the inside."**

–Luther Green

At times, you must be able to cut deeper into yourself

and others to see if your inner spirit is in alignment with

what you are displaying on the outside. You must be

willing to look deep within yourself to prepare yourself

for greatness. You cannot judge others for

uncleanliness when your own life is unclean and your

thoughts are dirty.

Second, will you be strong enough in your faith to not be shaken by people? You should not be afraid to step out on your own and away from the crowd to do what is right. People who are on your side will always be trying to push you forward, not hold you back. God gave you a gift. Whether it is being athletic, kind, or good at math; don't waste that gift just to impress people or fit in. There are people who will try to bring you down and steal your greatness. These are people who see your power and want what you have. For example, if you are a virgin and saving yourself for marriage, that is a gift from God for your spouse. The devil will try to steal that virginity by sending you someone who only wants you just because you still have your virginity, which makes you exclusive. This is so prevalent that God used Solomon to describe this person perfectly in the following passage in the Bible.

27

Proverbs 4:16-19 states,

"For they sleep not, except they have done mischief;
and their sleep is taken away, unless they cause
some to fall. For they eat the bread of wickedness,
and drink the wine of violence. But the path of the
just is as the shining light, that shineth more and
more unto the perfect day. The way of the wicked is
as darkness: they know not at what they stumble."

In this passage, it directly states that people will not rest and will try to find a way to make you fall, quit, or lose faith. Wolves in sheep's clothing are everywhere. Some are closer to you than you think: next to you on the bus, in front of you in class, or even the reflection in the mirror. Devils in disguise invite drama and bask in

knowing that you would please man over God.
Individuals not grounded by faith will be quick to start
a fight but slow to forgive or not forgive at all. Will you
recognize these people before it's too late?

You must ask God to reveal the motives of others.
You cannot wait until you are punched or arrested for
someone else's crime. God forbid there is a gun
pointed in your face to finally make you see the danger
of keeping company with the wrong people. You know
who these people are right now in your life, those who
are taking you for all your worth and bleeding you dry.
You don't want to end up living in Hell because you co-
signed a lease (your life) with someone who has prime
property next to the lake of fire (Hell).

Third, will you set goals, set priorities, and have standards? You are defined by the company you keep. If you are friends with people who do drugs and you don't, it doesn't matter because you will be guilty by association. Do not allow people to dictate whether you are going to be successful or not. Remember who you are and what you stand for. Don't give that up for anyone who will cause you to be less than great. No one can make you feel bad unless you allow them to. People who are after your joy and peace are just dead weights in your life. These are the people who are unmotivated, have no vision for the future, and have no ambition. These people are the walking dead in their spiritual graves. Enabling others to wear you down jeopardizes your own ability to unlock your true potential.

In truth, "haters" are trying to pull you down just as hard as you are trying to help them up. You must rise above the sins of others and claim your freedom. You must live your own life. You must be a symbol for righteousness. You are your own brand, and you must live a transparent life of greatness from the inside out. There is only one you! This is what the devil is after. Value your life and do not give yourself away freely. Why would you keep connecting yourself to things that diminish your worth? Don't sell yourself short! Our Lord and Savior bought you with His life to show you just how much you are worth. If God can see it, then it's time for you to see it too!

Did you ever have to turn down your music in the car just so you could parallel park? That is how you can realize who is for you and who is against you. In order to be able to reach your goals, you have to be able to turn off the static and ground noise (step away) so you can concentrate on what you have to do. There will be some things (people) you cannot simply turn down or tune out—you must turn these people OFF. You must break free from the sins of others. The God in you is stronger than the world around you. Never let the world put chains on you.

"If you want a life with no chains, then you cannot continue to keep connecting yourself to the chain gang."

–Luther Green

God cannot free you from the bondage of people who are no good for you if continue to associate yourself with people who are dead weights. You are

NOT the missing link. You are the chain breaker! If you are seeking God's instruction, there are times when you will be required to separate yourself and listen quietly so you can hear the voice of God with clarity.

Sometimes, you can be so caught up in desires of the flesh that you cannot see that you are walking into a trap. Some of the trials that you went through could have been avoided if you just paid attention to the warning signs God sent you. God sends you signs through dreams, temporary setbacks, or other people. God always gives you an opportunity to turn around in order to protect you from harm. Unfortunately, many ignore the big red flare blazing in the middle of the road. That red flare is reminding you that Jesus died for you, and his blood already cleansed you from the sin you are about to commit. If God can speak through a burning bush or even a donkey, then surely He can use someone else to warn you that you are headed down the wrong path. Life is too short to be making every mistake yourself. Learn from others and save yourself the heartache.

Lastly, you must also know and acknowledge that you were created for greatness. Don't let anyone keep you from unlocking your true potential and being all God intended you to be. God will give you the POWER to defeat every situation in time. Be strong in this journey. You don't have to be knocked over anymore. Stand on your own if you have to. If you are trying to reach that greatness, you have to know what to hold on to and what to let go of. You cannot hold the hand of the devil and then raise the other hand up to God, telling Him how much you love Him. You cannot brag about how God delivered you from destructive activities in your life while you are out at the bar with a beer in your hand. God doesn't operate like that. You cannot be a Christian and have close friends who do not go to church. You cannot go to breakfast with God then turn around and meet the devil for lunch! You have to be strong enough to let go of people in your life who contradict your destiny.

1 Corinthian 10:21 States:

"Ye cannot drink of the cup of the Lord, and the cup of Devils; Ye cannot be partakers of the Lord's table, and the table of Devils."

You cannot play both sides. If you want stability in your finances, jobs, and relationships, do you not think God wants to see some stability of Him in you? Remember, stability is your ability to stand strong in your gifts and values, even when the world around you is attempting to push them down.

Bad habits are hard to break, which is quite a conundrum because good habits are the ones that sustain you. Good people can have bad habits. They can have things inside of them that are not in the will of God. Good people can get angry, be in love with the wrong person, or have trouble letting go of the pain that someone caused them years ago.

Proverbs 26:11,

"...even a dog returns to its own vomit."

That is no different when God frees you from the destructive people in your life. The people who stole from you, cheated on you, and walked all over you are still on your "favorites" list in your cell phone. You must see these people as getting in the way of your own progress. They are distractions that will lead to your destruction. This fact is hard to swallow, but some people will send you straight to your grave. The devil will certainly tempt you. When you are thirsty, hungry, or lonely, you must pray for wisdom and not eat, drink or partake in the first good-looking person placed in front of you. Temptations are a slippery slope to trouble and need to be avoided at all costs. God gave

Eve to Adam, but it was Eve who was tempted by the devil in the Garden of Eden. Eve convinced Adam to eat the forbidden fruit. Even if God gives you someone or something, you must still trust the commandments of God over man. No matter what the source, it must line up with God's word first. You cannot put more trust in a person than you do in God.

Think back and look at how far you have come. People tried to take you out, tried to break you, and tried to make you quit. Well, guess what? You are still standing! In the end, it is far better to stand alone with hands stretched to up to God than to be holding hands with the devil on the path to darkness and destruction. It is time for a change! It is time for you to see that you will always have people trying to knock you down and diminish your worth, but you can stand tall in the refreshing power of God. Once you break free from your enemies, you will be catapulted ahead past all the people who tried to stop you. You will be transformed inside-out with a velocity, power, and intensity you have never seen before!

Take a long look at yourself, and think about where you want to be and where you are at now. Even if you are in a bad place, all you have to do is decide to step up on that rock and reach both hands up to the Heavens and towards God. Let go of the people who are dragging you down. Let go of any feelings you have for people that are not benefitting your life in a positive way. Get ready to move the dark clouds out of the way because you were born to shine.

Chapter Four –

Intentional Intentions

Excuses allow people have a stockpile of intentions but an empty space of broken dreams. There are many things we envision and set out to do in this life. In order to reach your destined level of greatness, you must move your speech into action. People will judge you by your actions, not by your intentions. People may doubt what you say, but can they doubt what you do?

Whether it is a birthday, special holiday, or start of a new season, you will create a new list of intentions.

When these goals are unfulfilled, it's not because you physically cannot complete them; rather, it's all the excuses you use not to follow through with what you said you were going to do. With every intention, there is an excuse as to why it didn't get done. Anyone can say what they want to do or what they intend to be, but the people who actually reach their goals show that they are ready to embrace greatness. Refuse to allow your goals to lay dormant on the ground. Set your goals higher, and share your goals with God. Be accountable for your goals. Your intentions should be soaring into the heavens.

Intentions to lose weight, stop being angry, get to work on time, get out of bad relationships, or even start going to church are good intentions that you determine mentally. But what happens after you determine your

intentions mentally? Will there be any lasting
movement to follow up what you intend to do?

Intentions truly don't mean anything. Intentions
are just words, and unless you put some movement into
those words, nothing worthy will happen. There is
power in people who say they are going to do
something and get it done. There is also power in
finishing what you set out to do. People will gravitate to
someone who stands by their words. You cannot
succeed unless you finish what you set out to do.

Luke 14:28-30 states,

"For which of you, intending to build a tower,

sitteth not down first, and counteth the cost,

whether he have sufficient to finish it? Lest haply,

after he hath laid the foundation, and is not able to finish it, all that behold it begin to mock him, Saying, This man began to build, and was not able to finish."

Sometimes, you are just juggling too many things at once and cannot apply the needed commitment and focus necessary to successfully complete a single task. That's the main reason why many people don't accomplish goals. Break it down, roll up your sleeves, and get to work. If you have to take it day-by-day or hour-by-hour, that's fine. At least you are moving in the right direction. Have your whole heart into what you are doing, and never leave a job undone. Make sure that you are equipped and ready before you make the commitment to do something.

It's not about what you say; it's about what you *do*. You might have been in a relationship where your partner treated you badly and failed to live up to their promised expectations. Maybe your partner said he would provide for you, but instead he is living off of you. Maybe she said she has your back, but the second you say something she doesn't like, she runs. He said that he would marry you, yet he keeps coming up with excuses for why you're not sporting a rock right now.

Understand that whatever you say will be written next to your name. Your character and personality will be judged by your words and whether or not you follow through with those words. Your words cannot be hollow; they have to be filled with a promise! So how many careless words have you released from your mouth? How many words did you leave behind without manifesting them into something great? Your words are important because that is what's going to define who you are to other people.

It's an ongoing cycle. Realistically, some of only the intentions that people will follow through with are the ones that only benefit them in the moment. How about the intentions a person has who is lusting after you to get you to bed? They will pull out every reason in the book to get you to drop those pants and satisfy their momentary needs. Then once they do, here come the excuses for why they just aren't ready for a relationship yet. In some cases, people will work so hard at the goal of tearing someone or something down but will not have time to build something or someone up.

Truthfully, there is a lot of work to be done. Some people have intentions to start going to church, but they claim they have to get their lives right before they can come. Sorry, but that is just another excuse to not go to church. Why wouldn't you go somewhere that will benefit you spiritually, financially, and mentally? Honestly, did it take you five years to get ready to go to the club or five minutes? Again, it's all about that momentary gratification.

Intentions without actions eventually become too heavy to carry. If something is important to you, you will find a way to get it done. How can this get done, you say? First, realize how important it is to do what you say you are going to do. Following through with your intentions allows you to be responsible, accountable, and trustworthy. Responsible people are trusted, and trusted people are responsible. You must be careful with your words because there is someone who may be counting on you to follow through.

Martin Luther King, Jr. had a dream, and he verbalized that dream in front of thousands of people. People counted on his dreams and words to come to fruition because their lives depended on it. His intentions changed the whole country because they weren't just words; the words were alive in his everyday life. His words were on display every time he left his front door, kissed his children goodnight, and prayed for strength from God. There was intentional power behind his words!

In the First Book to the Corinthians, chapter 4 verse 20 states:

"The kingdom of God is not in word, but in

Power."

This verse states that you cannot see words (intentions), but you can see actions (Power). So if God just intended to save you but never followed through on it, where would you be? What if God acted the same way you do, and when you asked Him to save you, He said "yes" but then never got around to doing it? He intended to, but it just was not high on His list, or He told you He will do it when He gets the time. Thank God that you have a Savior who doesn't just give you words but demonstrations of those words. God does what He says He's going to do, and it's always on time.

God intended to save His people, so He sent Moses to lead them out of Egypt. God also intended to save YOU, so He sent His son Jesus to lay His life down for you. Returning back to the Scripture in this chapter, if the Kingdom of God isn't in words (intentions) but in power (actions), then why do you seem to think that it's acceptable to not follow through with your promises? God's actions always speak louder than words. His intentions for your life will never come back void!

Intentional intentions are just as repetitive as your words when your words have no action behind them. Your actions will communicate your true feelings and intentions. Whether its personal intentions or promises to other people, make it a point not to make excuses for why you are not conquering what you set out to do. Make some real promises right now! Prove to everyone that your words and intentions are followed by actions.

Finish everything that you start the same way God is going to finish His great work inside of you! Words will show your interest, but actions show your commitment! Greatness is simply an opportunity to reach higher than you have ever before and to become somebody that nobody gave you a chance to be. Do not allow unfulfilled words to stand in your way of creating greatness in your life. Remember, actions speak louder than words.

Chapter Five –
Commitment to Greatness

You are now standing up, and it is a new day.
Faith is radiating from your body with such a vibrancy that you are shining through those dark clouds with a new passion, motivation, and power that you never knew was inside of you. In order to walk in this amazing power, you must be committed to it. Without 100% commitment, this gift will never flourish to the magnitude that God intends. Commitment is what moves your words into action. When you are committed to greatness, you are empowered to do the work rather than look for permission.

Being committed to greatness allows you to have the power to change things not just in your life but in the lives of others. Commitment involves accountability. Being committed and accountable to yourself and to others brings satisfaction to your actions. Accountability is a form of trustworthiness. If you are someone who possesses this, understand that you are a role model. You don't blame others for your mishaps; you just keep pushing through. You are accountable for what you say and what you do. You must understand that where you are from or what you are going through is supposed to be a testimony, not an excuse. You are accountable not only to yourself but to everyone around you. When you are committed, you are either in or out, hot or cold, focused on going to heaven or content to be going to hell. You are one or the other. Being committed to greatness means that you will be looked upon as a leader, and you are not afraid of that responsibility.

"God implanted within me a deeper understanding of what it means to lead and walk in greatness when I heard my spiritual mother, Prophetess Sheila Harris, preach in church." True leaders understand that their lifestyle is going to be watched and analyzed by everyone in their "flock." You cannot make a mistake or fail because your failure may be the destruction of someone else's hopes and dreams. More importantly, your failure would give others an excuse to use against you. At times, leadership is about helping others overcome life's obstacles.

Luke 12:48 states,

"For unto whomsoever much is given, of him shall be much required: and to whom men have committed much, of him they will ask the more."

At times, people may not like you because of your commitment, accountability, and standards, but leadership isn't about being liked; it's about getting people to the next level. As a leader, the people you are leading will need helped, saved, mentored, and guided, among other things. If you slide off track by doing something that you shouldn't do as a leader, then everyone may follow suit. You are a solid rock, and if you start rolling downhill, others who count on you may also slide off and roll with you. It is important to commit to doing right.

You must become the person you are trying to empower people to be! You cannot just be committed when it's convenient. You cannot just be great when you are in front of people or when you think you are being looked at. You cannot only be committed when you are on top or if it's sunny outside. Committing to greatness means being great even if life is not going your way. You have to show greatness even when no one is watching. People who are committed to something pursue it passionately, whether they are alone or in front of millions of people.

You will be watched by those who look up to you, regardless if you want to be or not. It is time to be the evidence and start providing living proof of what greatness looks like. The past is behind you now. You have been clothed in greatness. Every day when you wake up, you need to put it on and wear it! When you are clothed in greatness, trust that people are going to notice what you are wearing.

"Don't be blind to the fact that you could be someone else's celebrity." –Luther Green

Your actions should be living examples of how to treat your spouse, your children, and others. You must fully commit to greatness from the inside out. You must behave as if someone is always watching you. Greatness is a learned behavior. What are people learning from watching you?

What made you want to try smoking, have sex before marriage, or even learn to ride a bicycle? You most likely saw someone else do it first and thought it would be fun or cool. Most decisions you make in your life are based upon something you witnessed or heard. You must understand and remember that others (most importantly, children) watch what you do. How you respond to situations and how you approach circumstances is very important. When you portray the characteristics that you want others to possess, people will see the level of your commitment, and you will motivate others to greatness.

You must act like a champion if you want to become a champion or empower someone to be a champion. If you are saved and believe in God, then act like you are saved and believe in God. Someone may need to see the God in you to in order to navigate a storm. If you are acting like a loser, then you have already lost the game or the match. If you are making people around you feel like they are living in Hell, then you are showing that you live there also. Remember, some people (especially youth) may not follow your lead because they do not seeing anything in you that impels them to move. Your actions must give someone a reason to dream and reach higher.

Greatness is contagious, and it is a powerful responsibility. There are many people who dream of being a coach or mentor, but they do not truly understand the responsibility set before them. Being a coach, mentor, or leader is more of a calling than a job. It is a blessing, a gift not meant for anyone seeking to be famous. When you are gifted in leadership, your

God-given abilities allow you to be a breaker and a mountain mover. You have the empowerment to create hope, power, and desire deep within one's soul. Greatness is about being humble and never about gratifying "you." Leaders who walk in greatness understand when to apply the training wheels and when to take them off.

"The most powerful weapon you can give people is to open their eyes to a positive future, no matter their present circumstances." --Luther Green

Teach others the will to succeed by any means necessary. Allow others to feel important, and show that you are there to inspire greatness. As a leader, you should never be defeated or afraid to fail because failure leads to progress. When tough times come, lead by example and show that you are steadfast and immovable. A leader's responsibility is to push potential and empower people to reach their goals. As a leader, you must stand out from the crowd.

You are special, and you are an amazing creation. If that wasn't true, God wouldn't have given you the power of greatness and the ability to make that power grow infinitely. People who are committed to greatness are set apart from everyone else.

Having high standards will always give you and those associated with you the ability to always expect the best out of each other. High standards bring you to a point where you are not afraid to be bold because you are determined to get to where you are going. Boldness in your commitment to greatness enables you to speak the truth and to perform a task without fear of consequences, simply because you know that it's the right thing. Boldness in your commitment means recognizing that God is on your side. It's the ability to stand up and do the right thing at the right time. This will also allow you to be disciplined with yourself and your actions. You cannot be committed to greatness but continue to accept low standards for everything else around you. Having high standards and a high level of commitment is a must in order to move forward in any aspect of your life. You must be committed and accountable in order to create greatness, not just for yourself but for others. Remember, people will see the fruit that your commitment produces. That job will be

yours, your finances will increase, and your

relationships will improve! Being committed is not just

a word: it is a powerful and strategic MOVE to be so

much greater than you have ever been before!

Chapter Six –

Transcending Greatness

Once you have awakened the power of greatness for yourself, it's time to help the next generation to do the same. Transcending your greatness is one of the greatest actions you can do for someone else. God gave you this "gift" of greatness without asking you to pay Him back. That is the true definition of a "gift." God has gifted every man, woman, and child with special abilities, strengths, and talents. God didn't do that so you could flaunt them but for you to use them to help others. Your gift is meant to be shared and given back to the next generation. Now it's time for your light to give life to the next generation so it can be replenished and prosper. In order to transcend your greatness, you must rise above and go beyond this moment; you must look into the eyes of the future and plant the seed of greatness before it's too late.

Proverbs 13:22 states,

"A good man leaves an inheritance to his children's children."

You should be passing down things that will sustain future generations and help maintain their greatness. You cannot empower youth by condoning fighting, drinking, smoking, or promiscuity. Show them how to find and use their gifts. Show them that they are priorities in your life.

#CREATEGREATNESS

So when was the last time you asked your parents for advice? How many years ago did you laugh until your stomach hurt from one of your grandparent's "When I was your age" stories? When was the last time you prayed for a family member when they were not sick or hurt? When was the last time you just prayed for someone because you loved them? These moments are happening less and less. We don't talk; we "tweet." We don't fellowship; we "Instagram." We are missing the very moments in which knowledge, respect, and wisdom are passed down from generation to generation, and we must take action to transcend and create future greatness.

Greatness is what you leave behind for the next generation to pick up and use. You cannot be content with just being happy that your life is good. You have to care about the happiness of the lives that are connected to yours. What if God was as selfish as this generation is? Would He have sent his son to die for your sins on that Cross? What if Jesus never picked up His Cross and said, "No, I'm not laying my life down for them." What if He had the same selfish spirit you have and said, "I don't feel like answering prayers today, nor do I feel like healing today... I'm too tired." What if God's answers back from your prayers was, "What have you done for me lately?"

The world is changing, and people seem more concerned with passing their flesh than their faith. When men and women have to walk around half naked to get noticed, then there is a need to reevaluate individual self- esteem! Women, how can you walk around with all of your body parts showing and then complain that men only want you for your body and not your mind? Why is it that men know how to match their boxers to their shoes, their shoes to their watch, and their watch to their earrings, yet they can't even tie a tie for a job interview! You feel that it is important enough to dress up for a date to satisfy your flesh, but it's not important enough to dress up for church to satisfy and cleanse your spirit for God! You must pass on your faith to the next generation. Share with them not only the works of God but also the word of God. That will provide them the building blocks to navigate a world that is a lot tougher than what it was a decade ago. Transcending greatness asks the question, "What are you contributing to the next generation, and is your lifestyle sustaining it or draining it?"

The difficult thing to realize is that one day this generation will be called to lead countries, states, cities, congregations, teams, and families of the future. You cannot stop planting for the future, and you cannot stop nourishing the next generations. Without nourishment, the next generation will continue to degenerate and decay. The erosion of morals is manifesting itself and hardening hearts towards one another. This new generation is physically, mentally, and spiritually killing sons and daughters. Society places trust in a prescription of a pill instead of the deliverance of self-discipline. Instead of teaching one another to do right, we make excuses for one another to do wrong. The next generation now dreams of becoming professional sports players instead of doctors, rappers instead of teachers, playboy bunnies instead of mothers, and sperm donors instead of fathers. There are people

so desperate for companionship that they will give a
stranger the key to everything only after a few hours or
days.

What happened to morals and standards for life?
This generation is all about SELF, and you are a part of
this generation. Will you continue to keep everything
for yourself, or will you give back to the next
generation? You cannot live your life centered on
pleasing your body and not caring about the
consequences. Is that the best you can offer this
generation? You must be willing to sacrifice the "feel
good" moment in exchange for a "feel great" eternity.

Having personal integrity will drive you to want
more for yourself and the people you love. If you're a

mother who's showing your teenage daughter how to dress and act sexy, then you are setting her up to get her heart broken. The first man she does that for will only want or see one thing when they see her: SEX. If you are a father who accepts that your son is drinking to the point of violence and aggression, then you're setting him up to beat his wife! Personal integrity does not make excuses for anything that may hurt, destroy, or corrupt, no matter how cool, funny, cute, or harmless you think it may be at the time. You must direct your integrity while you still have the strength and power to keep future generations on the narrow road to greatness. Your voice, actions, and standards provide the nourishment that generations will need to survive long after you are gone.

Proverbs 22:6 states:

**"Train up a child in the way he should go: and
when he is old, he will not depart from it"**

One of the first words you learned as a baby was
NO. Why is it so hard for you to say NO to situations
and people that persuade you to do bad things? Let's
say, for example, that you are lonely and say "yes" to
the first person who shows interest in you. What
happened to NO? People who have the flu or a cold are
avoided like the plague, yet people will meet someone
at a bar or online, have casual sex, or even move in
together only after a few months or weeks.

Loneliness is a mind-state, not a disease. There is

no special drug, man, or woman out there that is going to cure your desire or fear of being alone. Greatness is not measuring your self-worth on how many "likes" and "followers" you have on social networks. Greatness is finding solitude in actually helping yourself and others in real life. Seeing abundance and strength in physical and spiritual form allows you to transcend greatness. You are accountable for right now, but you are also accountable for the next generations.

Many mentors witness youth saying how "grown up" they are, yet they don't know how to pay a mortgage or even walk a day in the shoes of an adult. The youth are in such a hurry to be free from their parents but have no idea how to get a job and live on their own. The decaying of the generations has attributed to this because adults are acting like teens. They have the impression that they're mature, but they certainly are not! Adults don't wear their pants down below their backside, and conflicts do not end with threats and fists flying. Maturation means that as you grow, your needs, tastes, and expectations should all change.

God blessed you to be a parent or a mentor and to give back to the next generation. God performed one of the greatest miracles you have ever experienced by creating a life inside of you or by having a life look up to you. Are you ignoring your miracle? Are your children spending more hours playing video games and searching Google rather than asking for your advice on relationships and sex? It is your duty to arm yourself with wisdom and values that will guide the next generation to grow and mature. Spend time with this generation. Protect this generation long enough so it can develop morally and avoid contamination. This is the generation you will leave behind. Examine yourself right now. What will the next generation take from your life long after you are gone?

Greatness is providing the next generation with the TRUTH, instructing them on how to find and use their gifts. With so much of our lives revolving around a "virtual world," you must give young people something real that they can reach out and touch. The truth is, if you're not giving back to the next generation—you are stealing something from it.

The future is watching you. Greatness is not given to you just so you can take over the world and "do you." Remember, you must pass down more than just your last name. This generation will learn from the faith that you show. Teach the next generation that they are important. Demonstrate to the future what it means to trust God over the world around them. Show them that their bodies are worth protecting, their minds are their gifts, and their spirits can be powerful forces that can go beyond what they see right now.

Chapter Seven – Sustaining Greatness

You have now built a foundation of greatness based upon the rock of your faith. The time is now. Don't just walk in the power of greatness for a moment; sustain it for an eternity. The power to take charge of your life and future is in your hands right now, but the question is, do you have the endurance to keep this living, breathing power of greatness alive? Do not put it off for another moment or wait for another sign from God. This is your destiny. It is your destiny to provide, support, and confirm the power of greatness inside of you. From the moment you picked this book up, you have grown stronger and stronger in the greatness that God provided you with. You have enough strength to uphold your greatness inside.

Understand that there is power in inspiring others, just

like you were inspired. With God, you have the strength

inside to maintain everything that makes you great.

In order to validate your greatness, you will have to

make it a priority every day. Do not be overwhelmed.

Break it down and perfect it piece by piece. Even

though greatness is something that is planted inside of

you, it still needs cultivated and watered for it to grow.

It is a process.

Learning discipline will defend every great action

you seek to perform. Set plans, goals, and rewards.

Have the determination to push forward. Just think

about what you will be able to accomplish, conquer, climb, survive, and change over the course of your life if you are truly determined in your goals and actions.

Chronicles 15:7 states:

"Be ye strong therefore, and let not your hands be weak: for your work shall be rewarded."

Be resilient. You are on an uncompromising mission, and you cannot be weak. You cannot just give up when things get tough. Anytime you are even thinking the word "QUIT," you need to replace that word with "PUSH!" Becoming resilient means that you have great character and that you have decided to

become immovable! Sometimes in life, you have to

adopt the spirit of Jacob in the book of Genesis 32:26

when he said,

"I will not let thee go, except thou bless me."

There are times when holding on to God's

blessings can be tough. Sometimes, you allow other

people to get in your way, or maybe you even get in

your own way. You have to use the greatness inside of

you to overpower anything that attempts to hinder your

growth. No matter what you are going through, do not

allow anything to block you from being great. If you

fall down, get back up! Remember, someone else may

need you to hang in there!

You must display an intensity for greatness in order to be able to maintain it. How can you keep a dream alive without passion and intensity? Passion and intensity are the sustaining powers behind greatness. You are not guaranteed another day, hour, or minute on Earth, so you must live each and every second like it could be your last!

Maintaining a vision for the future is vital to transcend greatness. You have to see yourself continuing to do great things. The same vision of "saving the world" that you had as a child should still inspire you as an adult. Never allow anything to dim the radiance of your vision.

"You can miss greatness because you spend too much time looking at your trials that you miss your triumphs."

--Luther Green

Let your actions be evidence that (1) God is real, (2) Everyone is important, and (3) No problem or situation can stop you if you sustain a passion to be great. As with everything, you always have a choice because God gave you the spirit of free will. The ability to choose is one of the greatest powers you can possess, and your greatest weakness is YOURSELF.

Ask God to give you the wisdom to accept the things that you cannot change and the faith to guide you with the things you (and God) CAN change. Pray daily because falling short just isn't acceptable for you anymore.

James 1:12 states:

"Blessed is the man that endureth temptation: for when he is tried, he shall receive the crown of life, which the Lord hath promised to them that love him."

Once people see the greatness shining from within, they will want to be around you more. People generally want to be around someone who makes them feel good. However, you need to have spiritual discernment to be able to identify those who want to learn from you and those who want to steal from you. Greatness is something that is extremely attractive. At times, you may feel stressed or stretched too thin, but that is just God wanting you to use your training so you can reach higher than you did before. Remember, there is always another level that you can reach during this journey.

In order to keep sustaining your gift of greatness, you must continue to keep God first. God has given you so much more than you give Him credit for. The sight in your eyes, the air in your lungs, and the blood that nourishes your body are all things God provides for us on a daily basis. You cannot fail to thank Him for it. God will always have your back, and He will always speak up just before you stop believing in the power He has given you. Have you ever noticed that the people who are diagnosed with a terminal illness but never believe it live longer lives than expected? How about the people who have no money but always have food on their table every night and clothes on their backs? That is God sustaining them throughout their journeys so that they can be testimonies to other people.

This is your journey, and it is far from being over. In actuality, it is just beginning. You can conquer any mission and not compromise the gifts that God gave you to use. Believe that you will sustain this gift of greatness! The power is in your hands to change lives for the better simply by refreshing, reviving, renewing, recharging, resisting, and repenting. Continue to fill your spirit with wisdom. Continue to read, and associate with people who have wisdom and passionately seek knowledge. Your thoughts, procrastination, or fear of standing out can no longer keep you bound.

Even though the road may be tough, you will look down from the heavens one day and see the fruits of all your labor. The greatness in you will give birth to the greatness in others who come after you!

God bless you, and always CREATE GREATNESS!

ABOUT THE AUTHOR

Luther Green Jr. is an educator, author, coach and motivational speaker that now lives in Harrisburg, PA. His passion is to use his God given gifts and life lessons to help others realize their true potential in life. Luther has been a keynote speaker at FCA (Fellowship of Christian Athletes) huddles and various other community outreach speaking engagements. He has been awarded multiple awards for leadership and continues to strive to motivate and inspire everyone he comes in contact with.